HABIT

Josie Boulding & Ryan Stuart

HABIT

6 Bases, 29 Recipes and a New Way of Cooking

Josie Boulding & Ryan Stuart

Restless Josie

—— COOKS ——

Josie Boulding & Ryan Stuart
HABIT

First Edition
Print ISBN 978-1-0688142-0-4
eBook ISBN 978-1-0688142-1-1

Food Photography & Styling | Josie Boulding
Cover Photography and Photos on Pages 5, 6, 12, 15, 17, 22, 24, 27, 28, 31, 32, 51-57, 63, 64, 79, 89, 105, 120 | Lou Dahl
Book Design | Lou Dahl
Editor | Jen Groundwater

This book is dedicated to our moms, who gave us a taste for healthy foods, and written for our daughter Paige, who will always be our favourite dinner companion.

CONTENTS

INTRODUCTION

HABIT / HAB·IT

A regular tendency or practice, especially one that is hard to give up.

The roots of this cookbook reach far and dig deep. Two of the sturdiest ones connect to our respective childhoods (read more about that on page 13). Another important one started during the COVID-19 pandemic lockdown. Other tendrils relate to allergies and health concerns, a shared interest in longevity and fitness, and a passion for knowledge and teaching. There are rootlets that came from social media and the demise of magazines. And there's my (Ryan's) bottomless appetite and Josie's interest in nutrition. But the root that extends the deepest is what we do three times a day – the habit of how we eat.

Habit #1: Read

Josie is a celiac and can't eat anything with gluten. Diabetes runs in my family, so I avoid sugar. Our daughter has several other food allergies. Rather than ruin our relationship with food, these complications encouraged us to build a healthier one. The first habit we developed was to read every label. Even healthy-looking prepared foods and sauces shocked us with copious sugar, preservatives and, especially, cheap and unhealthy oils. Many also turn out to hide unexpected allergens and ingredients.

Habit #2: DIY

It steadily became easier – and always healthier – to make our own sauces. Habit number two was born. Crafting food from scratch allows us to cut out the crap and use whole ingredients. They taste at least as good as store bought and do better things for body and mind.

Habit #3: Simplify

Of course, homemade is always going to take more effort than grabbing a bottle off the shelf. We don't always have the time or the motivation. That's where habit number three (and this cookbook idea) came from. We realized many of our favourite foods rely on common denominators: lemons, cashews, miso, soy sauce, fresh herbs and creamy dressing. If we could reduce our recipes to a few of these "bases" and make them ahead of time in quantity, we would save time and effort.

Habit #4: Prepare

A little kitchen experimentation later, we had our simple bases figured out and had tweaked a bunch of recipes to build off them. The addition of a few ingredients turns Cashew Cream into a creamy salad dressing or decadent dessert. Lemon Preserve makes a mean cocktail and a delicate white fish. Teriyaki is a starting point for a stir-fry and tacos. Once we developed the habit of having these bases in the fridge, dinner was never far away.

Habit #5: Make it easy

All these habits flirt with one of the most powerful productivity hacks around. Variety may be the spice of life, but we humans are creatures of ritual. Some are good and some are bad. The secret to nurturing more good habits is making them easier to do than the bad.

Our "bases" did just that. Preparing them ahead of time simplified grocery shopping and food prep. Having them in the fridge sped up cooking time and reduced food waste. Plus, they saved us money – healthy and gluten-free sauces are expensive!

Habit #6: Reinforcement

The habit was regenerative. Making it easier to make healthy food made it easier for us to eat healthy. The more we did, the better we felt and the more we wanted to eat healthy foods.

Some might call this a diet. We disagree. Dieting fails most people, most of the time, because depriving yourself is not a sustainable strategy for creating "a regular practice that is hard to give up." Instead, we like to think of this cookbook as the foundation for a healthier relationship with food. Its roots go deep and extend wide, holding us stable and strong, and nurturing health and happiness.

We've found this cookbook to be a habit that is easy to do, hard to give up and tastes delicious. We hope you do, too.

ABOUT US

Producing a cookbook and enjoying a marriage have a lot in common with making risotto. It's more work than anticipated, takes care, love and attention, and is best done with a glass of a white wine in hand. Oh, and is totally worth the investment. That's what we've found, anyway.

Many people are surprised to hear our marriage could handle making a cookbook together. There were definitely a few tense moments. But mostly it was a fun project that brought us closer together. Although we each have our silos in life, the kitchen has always been a happy place for us.

Josie, the photographer and chef

Josie grew up at Strathcona Park Lodge, a resort on Vancouver Island founded and run by her parents.

Food was always central to the Lodge experience. Their meals are famously healthy and nutritious – Josie's mom, a home economics teacher by training, was ahead of her time. Long before the dangers of a sweet tooth made headlines, her mom labelled the sugar bowl "white death." Josie's upbringing ingrained healthy food choices into her lifestyle, but it took food allergies and a pandemic to make it a priority.

Her first food allergy showed up when she was a kid. Other sensitivities followed. For a while she wasn't eating corn, tomatoes or milk. As one after another of her siblings went gluten free, Josie finally accepted her reality. About 15 years ago she ditched wheat. It took a while, but her health and digestion steadily improved and the other food allergies disappeared.

Meanwhile, the rest of Josie's life was focused on art. Before discovering her love for crafting in the kitchen, Josie worked as a professional photographer for many years. As still cameras onboarded video, so did Josie. She produced and hosted *Restless Josie*, a travel and lifestyle TV show that aired on ToughTV, Sportsnet and CHEK TV. She continues to play with both mediums, particularly on Instagram. Her @restlessjosie posts mix fashion, food, travel and lifestyle.

Josie returned to university in her forties and earned a Bachelor of Arts and Science with a focus on nutrition and psychology. The courses ignited her simmering interest in food. They taught her that you literally are what you eat and that nutrition influences mental health. But she also saw that eating more whole ingredients and less processed food was not easy, especially for those with food intolerances. An urge to help started to grow.

Ryan, the writer and eater

I'm the wordsmith side of this project and my interest in food is one part history and one part hungry.

When I was growing up, dinners were always an important family time. My mom made healthy food and we savoured it together. We sat down as a family every night. Some of my fondest memories are from the table and cleaning up afterwards.

I'm sure it didn't hurt that I was a hungry teenager and any meal time was prime time. I have always had a fast metabolism and an active lifestyle. I love to ski, climb, mountain bike, paddle, run, surf and hike.

All that exercise creates an appetite, enabling my second favourite activity: eating. I love good food. But I was never one to chow empty calories. Diabetes runs in my family, so I became aware of the link between sugary foods and my health earlier than most. Doing outdoor activities in challenging environments has provided me with firsthand experience about the link between what I eat and how I feel and perform, both physically and mentally. As I've gotten older, it's become even clearer.

My love of outdoor sports led me to Strathcona Park Lodge, which introduced me to outdoor guiding. From there I discovered my love of writing about my adventures. I've been a freelance magazine journalist for more than 20 years.

Ryan and Josie, the love story

We met while I (Ryan) was working at Strathcona Park Lodge teaching outdoor education. Our love of adventure was what brought us together initially, but we quickly discovered a shared interest in food and cooking. Just before we were married, we moved to the Comox Valley on Vancouver Island, an area known for its fertile farmlands and access to recreation. We've lived there ever since.

Our two passions – in the kitchen and in the wilderness – inform and influence each other in a feedback loop that eventually led to the idea for this cookbook.

In the early days of the COVID-19 pandemic lockdown, Josie was missing a connection with her community. She began filming herself cooking dinner and posting the videos to her Instagram feed. Occasionally at first, and then more and more often, I started manning the camera.

As the @restlessjosie audience grew, we started thinking about combining our skills to write a cookbook. We'd work on the recipes together – which would mean testing lots of food. I would write the recipe descriptions and the rest of the content. Josie

would tap into her photography skills to photograph the food – her eye is as sharp as her kitchen knives, and she takes great joy in turning food into art. It would be a husband-and-wife collaboration.

And that's just what we did. In a lot of ways, we've been working on this cookbook our whole lives. We hope you like the result.

LET'S KEEP IN TOUCH

If you have any questions, please get in touch with us. We'd love to hear from you.

Sign up for our newsletter: www.restlessjosiecooks.com
Follow us on Instagram: @restlessjosie

HOW TO USE THIS COOKBOOK

We don't like bossy ingredients or bossy cookbook authors, so we won't tell you what to do. But this is not your typical cookbook, so we will offer a few suggestions on how to make the most of the following pages.

FIRST, KNOW THAT EVERYTHING IS GLUTEN FREE, LOW IN SUGAR AND LIGHT ON DAIRY.

Where applicable, we've made note of possible allergen worries. This – together with simplifying the recipes as much as possible – sometimes means unusual ingredients. Flip the page to Ingredients & Substitutions to read more about why we made these choices and how to work around them. We've also made individual substitution suggestions throughout the book.

Now on to what makes Habit unique. We've broken the book into six chapters. Each one focuses on a different, easy-to-make base:

SALSA VERDE

TERIYAKI

MISO

CAESAR

LEMON PRESERVE

CASHEW CREAM

The first recipe in each chapter includes the instructions for making these base sauces. The rest of the chapter contains recipes for all the yummy things you can make with it.

For instance, the Salsa Verde Base makes salad dressing, risotto, quiche, pesto, mussels and enchiladas. With Lemon Preserve Base, you can create everything from a tequila cocktail to roast vegetables with a tahini sauce. We've included a fun chart on 23 that illustrates this structure.

Each base makes enough sauce to create two or three of its derivative recipes. And each base keeps for about a week in the fridge. In other words, make a couple bases on Sunday and you've already started a healthy dinner for every night of the week.

At the back of the cookbook is an index of recipes and ingredients. It's the fastest way to find your favourite meals or figure out what to make with the ingredients you've got in the fridge.

To be inclusive, we've kept spiciness to a mild-medium level and made a note for how to ramp it up or cool it off.

RECIPE
GUIDE

INGREDIENTS & SUBSTITUTIONS

If you want delicious food, start with good ingredients. This becomes even more true when you add a few restrictions, like gluten-free, nutritious and low sugar. Then when you try to simplify those recipes down to the shortest ingredient list and fewest steps possible, those ingredient choices become the difference between disappointment and delicious.

Our recipes and ingredient choices are the result of this kind of perfectionist trial and error. Think of them as a cheat sheet. We've done the hard work to make your cooking habits easier and your time in the kitchen more successful.

We've tried to keep the ingredients simple and easy to find. Even the more obscure ones should be available at your local health or natural food store. If not, Amazon carries every ingredient we use.

To explain our choices, we've gone into depth below and in some of the recipes.

Xylitol and sugar

Sugar adds flavour and extends shelf life to products, but does the opposite to us. Eating too much refined sugar is linked to obesity, diabetes and an increased risk of heart attacks and stroke. Xylitol is a naturally occuring sugar alcohol that is sweet like sugar but has 40 percent fewer calories and doesn't spike blood glucose. Compared to stevia, sorbitol and other alternative sweeteners, xylitol tastes more like sugar and is more digestible. Plus, you can exchange xylitol and sugar teaspoon for teaspoon.

Tamari and soy sauce

Soy sauce is a misnomer. Its main ingredient is actually wheat. It's tamari, which tastes similar to soy sauce, that's mostly made from fermented soybeans. Celiacs, and anyone else avoiding wheat, should read the labels on both. Unless specifically labelled gluten-free, most tamari and soy sauce contain wheat. When choosing between the two, we find tamari is less salty and a little richer, but the Asian-food staples are generally interchangeable.

Agar agar, guar gum and cornstarch

These are all thickening agents, used to make sauces less runny or to solidify an otherwise wobbly dessert. Agar agar is derived from red seaweeds. Guar gum comes from a bean. Cornstarch is refined from corn. For sauces we prefer agar agar's tasteless and less refined attributes. Cornstarch works as a 1 to 1 substitute. Guar gum is our go-to for desserts because it gives the best structure and doesn't need to be boiled to activate. If you prefer to use agar agar or cornstarch in place of guar gum, you will need to use six times as much to achieve similar results.

Miso paste

There are several different flavours of miso. All are made from soybeans, water, salt and, the key ingredient, koji. Koji is the cereal culture - whether soybeans, barley or rice - that yields a distinctive flavour and allows the miso to ferment. White miso uses a rice koji and ferments for the shortest time, giving it the mildest and sweetest flavour. Red miso, made with mostly soybean koji, is on the other end of the spectrum, with a bold flavour. Several other misos fall in between. We like the approachable white miso for our Miso Base, but stronger flavoured varieties work well in stews and soups.

Oils

Oils are essential to cooking, but, wow, do they have a lot of calories: about 16 times more than fruit, and more than five times as many calories as meat. When we add something so nutrient dense to our cooking, we do it with intention. Olive oil is probably the healthiest. It's full of healthy fats, antioxidants and anti-inflammatory agents. But it has a low smoke point, so we reserve it for salad dressings and cooking below 300°F. Butter is our second favourite oil because, well, it really does make everything better, including us. It's full of good stuff, in particular linolenic acid, an anti-cancer agent. Coconut oil is our go-to when we want a solid oil – and its tropical flavour. We often use it in dessert crusts. Our go-to oil for anything in the oven and most of our frying is avocado oil. It has one of the highest smoke points of any oil and has almost no flavour.

SALSA VERDE

BASE
SALSA VERDE

Makes 1½ cups | **Prep** 5 minutes | **Cooking** 0 minutes

4 cups parsley, loosely packed

¾ cup olive oil

¼ cup lemon juice

2 garlic cloves, minced

1 teaspoon salt

Summertime in a bottle. Green goodness. Parsley tonic. We played with a variety of names for this simple concoction and, for some reason, a Spanish theme stuck. The combination of parsley, lemon, garlic and oil does have a Mediterranean theme to it and the green sauce is as healthy as the eponymous diet.

Parsley is rich in Vitamin K, which is key to blood clotting and bone health. It has immune boosters like Vitamin C and other antioxidants. The recipe uses plenty of olive oil. People who consume lots of olive oil have a lower risk of dementia, cardiovascular disease and some types of cancer. Garlic and lemon are also superfoods, full of health benefits.

Adding to the reasons to use this sauce is that parsley is one of the easiest herbs to grow, available fresh year round and budget friendly. It adds a subtle, but noticeable punch of flavour and a vibrant green colour that's especially nice to see during the winter.

We think this zesty sauce is so delicious, easy and useful. The recipe ideas over the next couple pages just hint at the potential.

1. Add all the ingredients to a blender.
2. Blend until well combined but not completely smooth.
3. Use immediately or refrigerate for up to a week.

YOGURT DRESSING
SALSA VERDE

Serves 4 as a side salad | **Prep** 5 minutes | **Cooking** 0 minutes

3 tablespoons Salsa
Verde Base

¼ cup plain, plant-based yogurt
(or organic dairy yogurt)

1 tablespoon lemon juice

Salt and pepper to taste

Some salad dressings bite your tongue with vinegar. Others drown leafy greens in cream. Both are fine, and sometimes necessary, when the ingredients are tasteless. But when they are farm fresh and full of flavour, you want a dressing that's more subtle. This is that dressing.

It's tangy and herby, creamy and light. It goes well with any salad mix, but is especially good with fresh veggies and fruit, building on their natural flavours to create something greater than their parts

1. Place all the ingredients in a bowl and mix. Yup, it really is that easy.
2. Pour generously over a salad mix. We like it best with leafy greens with chopped-up carrots, cucumber and some fruit, like pears.

RISOTTO
SALSA VERDE

Serves 4 as a main | **Prep** 15 minutes | **Cooking** 50 minutes

4 cups mushrooms

1 onion, diced small

3 tablespoons olive oil

2 cups Arborio rice

1 cup white wine (pick one you like to drink)

3 cups chicken broth

2 tablespoons Salsa Verde Base

½ cup Parmesan cheese, grated

1 cup smoked salmon

Salt and pepper to taste

TIP

It's easy to create risotto variations. Just ditch the mushrooms and smoked salmon and add 1 cup cooked veggies or other ingredients (spinach, snap peas) right after the Parmesan cheese.

Josie never used to make risotto because she thought it was too hard to get right. Now she realizes she was wrong. It just takes patience: lots of stirring and slowly adding broth. Working hard for something is always satisfying, especially when the result is this delicious. If you've got a bit of time and forearm strength, Josie is convinced this creamy, rich and winey risotto is totally worth the effort.

1. Warm a large cast-iron skillet over medium heat. Add 1 tablespoon of olive oil and then the mushrooms. Mix well and then cook, stirring regularly, until soft. Remove to a bowl and set aside.

2. Add another tablespoon of oil. Heat the oil and then add the onion. Cook, stirring often, until the onion starts to turn translucent.

3. Add the rice to the onion. Stir to coat the rice in the oil (add more oil if it's dry). Continue stirring frequently as you brown the rice on all sides. This will take about 10 minutes.

4. Pour in the wine. Keep stirring regularly until almost all of the wine has evaporated.

5. Pour in ½ cup of broth. Stir until the liquid has nearly evaporated. Repeat, adding broth in ½-cup portions. After you've added a total of 2 cups of broth, begin tasting the rice to check for doneness. You want it to be al dente, firm but soft, with no starchy aftertaste or pasty feel in the mouth.

6. When nearly done but there's still some liquid, stir in the Salsa Verde Base. If it's dry, add ¼ cup more broth and bring to a boil.

7. Once the risotto is al dente and there's almost no water left, stir in the Parmesan, smoked salmon and salt and pepper. Heat again and then serve immediately.

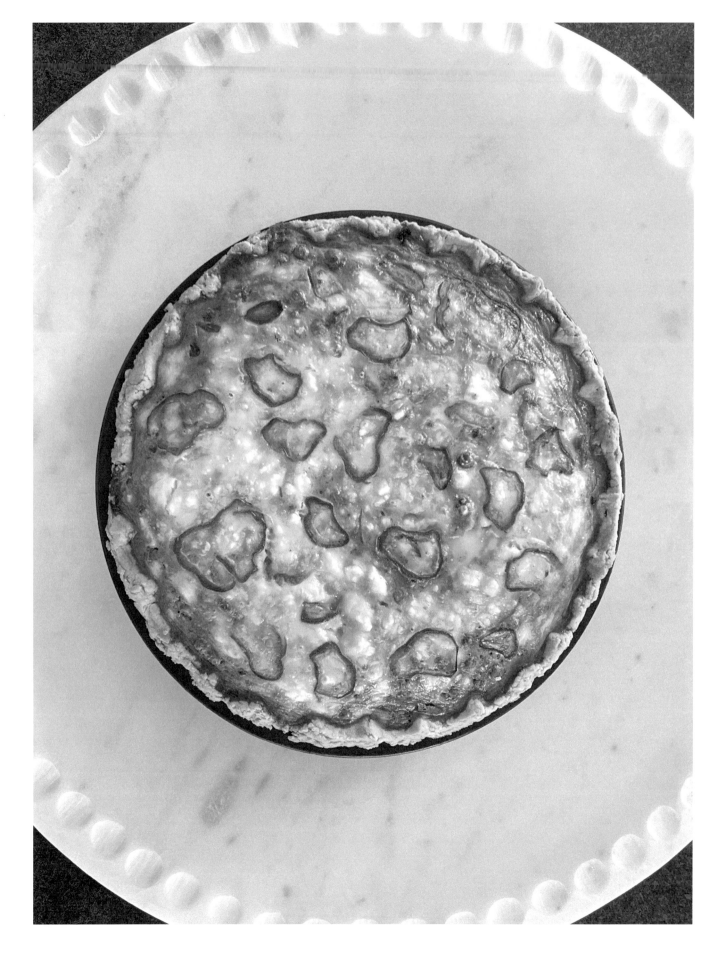

SPINACH AND FETA QUICHE
SALSA VERDE

Serves 6 | **Prep** 30 minutes | **Cooking** 15 + 25 minutes

FILLING

4 eggs

1 cup egg whites

½ cup steamed spinach, pressed to expel water

½ cup goat or sheep feta

1 tablespoon Salsa Verde Base

1 cup red pepper, chopped into rings

Salt and pepper to taste

CRUST

2 cups almond meal

3 tablespoons coconut oil

1 tablespoon everything bagel spice

¼ cup cold butter, grated

1½ teaspoon cold water

Josie rarely eats eggs before dinner. Meanwhile, I love eggs any meal of the day. This quiche satisfies us both. It's complex, filling and savoury enough for dinner, and I can eat the leftovers for breakfast or lunch.

We add the egg whites to lighten and add fluffiness, but the recipe works fine with four more whole eggs. The crust is our go-to recipe for a quick, gluten-free option, which contributes to the magic of this recipe. The impressive result looks challenging and time consuming, but it's actually faster than the recipe suggests and simple to whip together.

1. Warm oven to 350°F. Grease a pie pan.
2. Start with the crust by mixing almond meal with the oil and everything bagel spice.
3. Grate in the cold butter and add cold water. Mix well until it forms a ball.
4. Flatten the dough ball so it covers the pan up to the top of the sides, spreading with your hands to distribute evenly.
5. Pop the empty crust into the oven for 15 minutes.
6. While the crust cooks, prep the filling. Steam the spinach in a frying pan or pot with a tight-fitting lid (or thaw frozen spinach). Once spinach is thoroughly wilted and shrunken, cool and then squeeze out the excess water. Squishing with your hands is often the easiest way to do this.
7. Crack the eggs into a big bowl. Add egg whites and whip until well combined. Add feta, Salsa Verde Base and spinach. Mix well.
8. Remove crust from the oven and cool until just warm. Pour in the egg

recipe continues

mixture. You may need to gently move spinach and feta around to get an even distribution.

9. Add the pepper rings to the top and sprinkle with salt and pepper.

10. Put the pie in the oven and bake for 25 minutes more or until the egg mixture is solid. Check by poking the centre with a skewer. If it comes out wet, keep cooking.

11. We like it with hot sauce on the side.

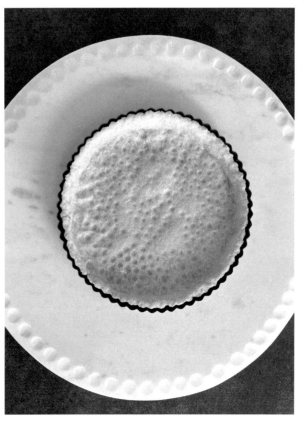

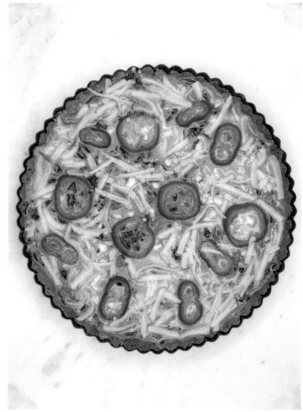

PESTO
SALSA VERDE

Makes 2½ cups | **Prep** 5 minutes | **Cooking** 15 minutes

½ cup Salsa Verde Base

½ cup Cashew Cream Base (see 107)

½ cup white wine (pick one you like to drink)

½ cup Parmesan cheese, grated

½ cup pumpkin seeds

TIP

Pesto freezes well. We like to use ice cube trays. Each cube holds about the right amount for one person's pasta.

Pesto is by far our favourite way to use Salsa Verde. Mixing the fresh herbs with nuts, seeds, wine and cheese creates a wonderfully balanced flavour that's pleasing to many palates and goes well with so many dishes: pizza and pasta sauce, of course, but also a topping for fish, chicken, veggies and salad.

The biggest difference between this recipe and the pestos at the store is the amount of oil. Store-bought pesto is usually dripping with it, while ours has very little, making it light and fresh. It also means you'll have to use a little more pesto than you usually would.

1. Heat a deep-sided frying pan on medium heat.
2. Once the pan is warm, add the Salsa Verde Base, Cashew Cream Base and wine. Stir to combine.
3. Continuously stir the sauce until the mix starts to boil. Turn the heat down to low and add the grated Parmesan.
4. Continue stirring until the cheese has melted into the sauce. If the cheese is being stubborn, turn the heat up a few notches to get it to melt.
5. Once the cheese is integrated into the sauce, add the pumpkin seeds and stir one more time. Serve immediately or store in the fridge for one week.

PEPITA CROUTONS
SALSA VERDE

Serves 3 big salads | **Prep** 15 minutes | **Cooking** 25 minutes

1 cup raw pumpkin seeds

2 tablespoons almond meal

2 tablespoons nutritional yeast

2 tablespoons olive oil

2 tablespoons red wine vinegar

1 tablespoon Salsa Verde Base

1 teaspoon dried basil

1 teaspoon rosemary

½ teaspoon salt

Croutons are not essential to a great salad, but they sure help. Sadly, gluten-free bread just doesn't have what it takes to become a dehydrated bread cube. Josie had almost given up on the wonderful crouton crunch until she discovered this surprising alternative. Baking a mix of pepitas (AKA raw pumpkin seeds), almond meal, nutritional yeast, spices and vinegar creates savoury and crispy nuggets that make croutons taste like, well, stale bread. As an added bonus, pepita croutons are full of iron and Vitamin C. They're enough to make almost any salad great again.

1. Warm oven to 325°F and line a cookie sheet with parchment paper.
2. Add all the ingredients to a food processor and blend for 1 minute. Stir and blend again for another 30 seconds. The goal is a well mixed, but still chunky, consistency.
3. Transfer the pumpkin seed mixture onto the cookie sheet, spreading evenly.
4. Bake for 10 minutes. Stir and bake again for an additional 10 minutes or until the top starts to turn golden brown.
5. Crumble and break up the pumpkin seed mix into smaller chunks.
6. Toss on a salad in place of croutons or just snack on handfuls.

MUSSELS
SALSA VERDE

Serves 4 for appetizers, 2 for dinner | **Prep** 5 minutes | **Cooking** 20 minutes

2 tablespoons butter

1 leek, chopped into thin rings, or 1 onion, diced

2 cups chicken broth

1 tablespoon Salsa Verde Base

¼ cup white wine (pick your favourite variety)

2 pounds mussels

We love mussels. They're delicious and nutritious. But it's more than that. Forking the meat out of the shell slows us down, forcing us to be present and savour each bite. We usually share them, so there's a social element. And there's the broth. Using a mussel shell to slurp up the liquid might be the best part.

1. Place a deep, heavy pot on medium-low heat. Melt the butter, then add the leek and stir to coat. Fry, stirring regularly, until the leek is fragrant and soft.

2. Add the chicken broth and Salsa Verde Base. Stir and turn the heat up to medium.

3. When the broth starts to boil, add the white wine and bring back to a boil.

4. Add the mussels to the broth. Stir and put a lid on the pot. You may need to turn the heat down to keep it at a simmer.

5. Check the mussels after three minutes. They are cooked when most of the shells open.

6. Serve immediately. Don't eat any unopened mussels.

GREEN ENCHILADA SAUCE
SALSA VERDE

Makes 1 cup | **Prep** 10 minutes | **Cooking** 10 minutes

1 tablespoon avocado oil

1 onion, sliced and diced

1 jalapeno, sliced,
seeds discarded

1 garlic clove

2 cans sliced green chiles

2 tablespoons Salsa
Verde Base

½ cup vegetable stock

1½ teaspoons cumin

½ teaspoon salt and pepper

Just another sauce that's good enough to drink. This one is a play on a Mexican enchilada sauce, which is traditionally poured over tortillas filled with meat and baked in the oven. The sauce works great for this, but we also love it as a substitute for salsa with quesadillas, tacos and tortillas, a dressing for salads and a sauce for chicken, pork or beef.

We rate it as a mild to medium spice. Use the amount of jalapeno to crank it up or dial it down. And if you find yourself without a fresh spicy pepper, pickled ones work nearly as well. Another option is to add a delightful smoky flavour by first roasting the jalapeno over an open flame. A margarita is almost a necessity at this point.

1. Heat a frying pan over medium heat. Add oil.
2. Toss sliced onion and jalapeno in the oil. Fry until the onion is translucent, about 5 minutes.
3. Mash the garlic into the cooking onions and jalapeno. Mix and fry for another minute or so.
4. Add the cooked veggies to a blender along with all the other ingredients. Blend on medium-high until the sauce is well combined, but still a little chunky.
5. Use immediately or keep for a week in the fridge.

TERIYAKI

BASE
TERIYAKI

Makes 1½ cups | **Prep** 10 minutes | **Cooking** 10 minutes

½ cup tamari or soy sauce

½ cup water

¼ cup honey

2 tablespoons rice vinegar

2 garlic cloves, pressed
(about 1 tablespoon)

1 tablespoon ginger,
peeled and grated
(about 1 small finger)

2 tablespoons lime
juice (about 1 lime)

¼ teaspoon agar agar powder
or cornstarch (see page 29)

TIP

If you're pressed for time, put
all the ingredients in a blender
(you can leave the garlic and
ginger whole), blend on high,
pour into a microwave-safe
bowl and microwave for 2
minutes.

Teriyaki is popular for the same reason people love caramel corn, salted chocolate and everything else that's sweet and salty. The two taste elements are perfect partners and are almost guaranteed to make anything taste good. However, store-bought teriyaki is usually full of sugar and bad oils and often hides gluten.

Luckily, making a healthy and gluten-free teriyaki is not hard and is good for you. Honey, fresh garlic and fresh ginger all have anecdotal and proven medical benefits and are rich in antioxidants and other helpful vitamins, minerals and nutrients.

You can use this recipe as is to marinate just about any meat. Just soak the protein in the Teriyaki Base for 30 minutes and up to overnight. Or check out our tweaks to turn it into all kinds of wonderful things.

1. Heat a frying pan on medium heat.
2. Add all the ingredients, except the agar agar, to the saucepan. Stir to mix well.
3. Now add the agar agar and whisk into the liquid, breaking up any chunks. Bring the Teriyaki Base to a boil.
4. Remove from heat. You can use it right away (say, in a stir-fry), but if you want to use it as a marinade, set it aside to cool and thicken first. After about five minutes, give it a whisk or vigorous stirring to prevent clumps.
5. Store in the fridge for up to a week.

STIR-FRY
TERIYAKI

Serves 4 | **Prep** 15 minutes | **Cooking** 20 minutes

1 onion, quartered and sliced

1 cup protein (we used chickpeas)

1 cup broccoli (cut up and separate stems from florets)

2 cups mushrooms

1 red pepper

1 cup snap peas

1 tablespoon peanut oil or avocado or coconut oil

½ cup Teriyaki Base

Stir-frying is one of the simplest ways of cooking. Doing it well is a different story. It demands one of the hardest-earned cooking skills – timing. That's because all ingredients cook at different rates. Tossing them all in at once leads to a Three Bears situation: overcooked, undercooked and just right, all at the same time.

Along with timing, to ace a stir-fry you also need another cooking skill – prepping. Cut all your ingredients the same size, dry them thoroughly and organize them into groups by hardness. Cook proteins first, followed by hard veggies (carrots, broccoli stems, cauliflower), medium veggies (mushrooms, peppers, broccoli florets) and finally soft stuff (cabbage, spinach, tomatoes). We make an exception to this rule. Because Josie leans towards a French style of cooking, we always start by sweating the onions.

Below are the steps and timing for a basic stir-fry. But now you have the formula to make it your own. Prep your ingredients and nail the timing, and the result will be so much better than a simple stir-fry.

1. Wash and dry the broccoli, mushrooms, pepper and snap peas.
2. Dice the onion.
3. Chop the other vegetables into bite-sized pieces and separate them into three piles: 1. broccoli stems; 2. broccoli florets, mushrooms and peppers; and 3. snap peas.
4. Heat a wok or deep-sided pan on medium-low heat. Pour in the oil, swirl to coat and then add the onion. Stir well. Cook, stirring often,

recipe continues

recipe continued from previous page

until the onion just starts to turn translucent.

5. Turn the heat up to medium-high. Add the protein. Continue cooking for two minutes.

6. Add the cut-up broccoli stems. Stir and cook until the stems start to soften, about 4 minutes.

7. Add the broccoli florets, mushrooms, and peppers. Mix well. Cook until the florets start to turn bright green and the mushrooms look soft, about 4 minutes.

8. Add the snap peas. Mix well and cook until the snap peas turn bright green, about 2 minutes.

9. Pour in the Teriyaki Base and mix well. Cook until the sauce is hot and steaming. Remove the wok from the heat.

10. Serve immediately, probably on top of rice.

SALMON
TERIYAKI-GLAZED

Serves 4 | **Prep** 10 minutes | **Cooking** 10 minutes

¼ cup Teriyaki Base

⅛ teaspoon agar agar powder or cornstarch

700 to 900 grams (1.5 to 2 pounds) sockeye or coho salmon fillet

TIP
—

The best way to defrost salmon is slowly. Transfer frozen fillets to the fridge at least 24 hours before you plan on cooking the fish. The slow defrost helps maintain firmer flesh.

Living on the coast of B.C., salmon is part of our culture. We cheer the tiny smolts as they dash towards the ocean in the spring, watch the west coast ecosystem feast on salmon all summer and marvel at the adults fighting their way upstream in the fall. They're so inspiring their likeness is everywhere, from team logos to town slogans. And we can't get enough of them: we snorkel with them, fish for them and, of course, eat them.

When fresh, salmon needs nothing more than a few spices and 10 minutes on the barbecue. A couple months in the freezer calls for more attention. Either way, teriyaki is a natural complement to the pink meat. You could use the Teriyaki Base as is, but we find it easier to work with when it's less of a sauce and more of a glaze.

1. Pour the Teriyaki Base into a microwave-safe bowl. Stir in the agar agar. Heat the mixture in a microwave in 30-second pulses, whisking in between, until it boils. (Alternatively, heat in a frying pan until it boils.) Set it aside to cool, either on the counter or in the fridge, to allow it to thicken into a gel. It should only take 5 to 10 minutes.

2. While you wait, heat a barbecue or oven to 400°F.

3. Wash and dry the salmon fillet.

4. Spoon or paste the teriyaki glaze over the salmon, covering all the pink parts. Transfer to the oven or barbecue.

5. Cook salmon until the thinnest part of the meat just starts to flake apart when poked with a fork. Cooking time will vary depending on the thickness of the fillet. Start checking after five minutes.

MUSHROOM TACOS
TERIYAKI

Serves 4 | **Prep** 10 minutes, plus marinating time | **Cooking** 30 minutes

2 cups mushrooms, sliced thick

1 red onion, sliced thin

2 tablespoons tomato sauce

⅓ cup Teriyaki Base

¼ cup avocado oil

1 tablespoon maple syrup

1 tablespoon cumin

1 tablespoon chili powder

1 tablespoon oregano

1 teaspoon cinnamon

½ teaspoon pepper

¼ teaspoon salt

NOTE

This may seem like a lot of marinade, but the mushrooms are so absorbent it will disappear.

This taco recipe makes the most of mushrooms' versatility. The fungi absorb so much flavour from this Mexican-themed marinade and then bake into a perfect chewiness, creating veggie tacos with a meaty feel, that are filling and incredibly satisfying. We love them.

Any mushrooms will work for this recipe, but we think a 50:50 mix of oyster and shiitake takes it to the next level. More important, though, is what you do with it. We like them best in a soft-shell tortilla (warmed in a frying pan) and topped with pickled onions, jalapeno peppers, some lettuce and sprouts. Even more important: sauces. A mango salsa goes well here, but even better is our Salsa Verde Enchilada Sauce (page 48) and Cashew Cream Chipotle (page 112).

1. Set the chopped mushrooms and onion aside. Mix everything else in a big bowl.

2. Add the sliced mushrooms and onion. Toss to coat. Refrigerate for 30 minutes to 24 hours.

3. Preheat the oven to 400°F. Line a baking sheet with parchment paper.

4. Spread the mushroom mixture across the baking sheet as evenly as possible.

5. Cook in the oven for 15 minutes. Flip the mushrooms. Return to the oven for another 15 minutes.

6. The mushrooms are done when they are soft and just starting to brown.

7. Add to tacos or salad and smother in condiments and sauces.

MISO

Base **65**

Creamy Veggie Soup **66**

Brown Butter Broccoli **69**

Buddha Bowl **70**

Peanut Sauce **73**

Spinach Gomae **74**

Mushroom Gravy **77**

BASE
MISO

Makes 5 cups | **Prep** 5 minutes | **Cooking** 10 minutes

4 cups water

½ cup miso paste

3 tablespoons tamari
or soy sauce

3 tablespoons honey

4 garlic cloves, minced

3 teaspoons crushed
dried chilies

¼ tsp smoked salt

TIP
—

There are several types of miso.
The difference comes down to
ingredients and fermentation
time. For this versatile base,
a mild-flavoured white miso
works best.

Our Miso Base is like a broth, but more satisfying, rich and interesting. We especially love to pair it with vegetarian dishes because miso is home to the fifth taste element, umami, which provides a meaty richness without leaving the vegetable aisle. That's just the start for this superfood.

Miso is usually a combination of soybeans, water and a fermented cereal called koji. Fermented foods are full of gut-health boosting probiotics, which help with digestion overall and, according to a growing pool of research, improve mental health, too.

Miso is also a good source of important nutrients and vitamins, including manganese, zinc, calcium and Vitamin K. The last one is key for vegetarians: Vitamin K is a building block for B12, an essential vitamin that's hard for your body to find without meat.

In our Miso Base, all those benefits come together in just a couple minutes. That's the definition of high reward for little effort.

1. Warm a small pot or wok over medium heat.

2. Once the pan is hot, add the water and miso. Stir or whisk until miso paste is fully integrated into the water.

3. Add the tamari, honey, garlic and chilies. Stir and heat until the Miso Base boils.

4. Take it off the heat and decant into a container. It will thicken when it cools down.

5. Store in the fridge for up to a week.

CREAMY MISO-VEGGIE SOUP
MISO

Serves 4 | **Prep** 30 minutes | **Cooking** 2 hours

1 tablespoon avocado
or coconut oil

1 onion, chopped
into small pieces

2 cups sweet potatoes
or squash, peeled and
cut into cubes

2 cups cherry tomatoes

2 cups Miso Base

¼ cup tahini

1 can coconut milk

1 teaspoon salt and pepper

1 teaspoon honey

One of the reasons we love autumn is soup. On the first cold, wet day in September or October, the soup switch flips and just like that, a warm, liquid meal, full of immune-boosting ingredients, is exactly what we crave. Rich, filling and complex, this is one of our favourites.

Don't feel constrained by our ingredient list: use any veggies that need to be used by frying them alongside the onion. We just recommend that the bulk of the soup be tomato and sweet potato/squash. They provide the heartiness to turn the cold and damp away.

1. For slow cooker, warm a frying pan on medium heat. Add the oil and onion and stir well. Fry the onion, stirring often, until it turns translucent. Transfer the cooked onion to the slow cooker along with all the other ingredients. Cook on the "high" setting for four hours or longer.

2. For stove top, use a heavy-sided pot and follow the same directions to cook the onion. Once the onion is translucent, add all the other ingredients to the pot. Once the soup boils, turn the heat to low and leave to simmer for one hour.

3. With both slow cooker and stove top: once the vegetables are soft, use a hand blender to cream the soup until chunks are gone and the soup is a uniform consistency.

4. Continue simmering until you are ready to eat. Serve with bruschetta or warm bread.

5. Refrigerate leftovers. It's even better the next day.

BROWN BUTTER BROCCOLI
MISO

Serves 4 | **Prep** 10 minutes | **Cooking** 20 minutes

1 large head of broccoli or 5-10 stems of broccolini

¼ cup butter

1 teaspoon dried and crushed chilies

⅔ cup Miso Base

TIP

Josie likes to use organic or grass fed butter. Farmers feed hormones to cows so they'll produce more milk, but excess hormones are considered a risk factor for some types of cancer. Like most animals, cows store hormones in their fat and milk, and thus butter is rich in fat. Organic and grass fed cows are fed fewer hormones.

We've had lots of veggie dishes that made us go "Wow!" Broccoli was rarely one of them. Until Josie plated this one. It may change your relationship with the overly healthy looking vegetable. You may, like us, even find yourself craving it.

This is definitely one of those occasions where butter makes it better. But the upgrade is also about process: roasting the butter-soaked broccoli in a hot oven caramelizes the sugars and fats. Take it to the next level by substituting in broccolini, broccoli's skinnier, wilder-looking cousin. We find it's a bit sweeter, especially when it's fresh from a local farm.

1. Preheat the oven to 400°F. Cover a cookie sheet in parchment paper.
2. Warm a frying pan over medium-low heat.
3. Chop broccoli into florets and cut the stem into similar-sized chunks. Place in a bowl.
4. Once the pan is warm, add the butter. When melted, add the chili flakes and Miso Base. Heat until the sauce just boils.
5. Pour the miso-butter over the broccoli and toss to coat.
6. Spread the broccoli across the cookie sheet, leaving room between each piece, and put it in the hot oven.
7. Bake for 10 minutes. Check the broccoli and continue cooking until it just starts to turn brown and a fork penetrates the stems with just a little pressure.
8. Best served hot.

BUDDHA BOWL
MISO

Serves 4 | **Prep** 15 minutes | **Cooking** 30 minutes

DRESSING

⅔ cup avocado oil

½ cup nutritional yeast

½ cup Miso Base

⅓ cup olive oil

⅓ cup rice vinegar

¼ cup water

3 tablespoons tamari
or soy sauce

3 tablespoons tahini

1 tablespoon fresh ginger

1 tablespoon peppercorns

BOWL

4 cups cooked rice
(any variety works)

1 tablespoon avocado
or coconut oil

1 block firm tofu, cut
into ½ -inch cubes

4 cups of veggies, cut into
bite-sized chunks (we like
carrots, cucumber, shelled
edamame and a red pepper)

1 avocado, sliced into chunks

¼ cup pecans, chopped

¼ cup pumpkin seeds

Our daughter turned us onto the convenience of bowls like this one. When she moved into her first apartment, she found they were a quick and delicious way to eat healthy foods. They're also versatile: combine just about any assortment of rice, veggies, maybe meat and a sauce. Dinner done.

The Buddha Bowl is our favourite version, mostly because the sauce is so good. The dynamic duo of nutritional yeast and Miso Base gives it a tangy depth we can't get enough of. Both ingredients are rich in vitamins and minerals, too.

1. Cook rice according to the package directions.

2. Combine all the dressing ingredients in a blender. Blend on high until smooth, consistent and thick but still pourable. If it's too thick, add water, a spoonful at a time, to make it runnier.

3. Set aside dressing. (You can store it in the fridge for up to a week.)

4. Heat oil in a wok or large frying pan over medium heat. Add tofu. Turn and stir tofu until all sides are lightly browned. Remove and set aside.

5. Add pecans and pumpkin seeds to the frying pan. Roast, stirring regularly, until fragrant and lightly browned, about 5 minutes.

6. Into four big bowls, place one cup of rice and about one fourth of the vegetables, nuts and seeds and tofu.

7. Pour a tablespoon or so of Buddha dressing on top of each bowl. We like to put extra on the table, mostly because we can't get enough.

PEANUT SAUCE
MISO

Makes 1½ cups | **Prep** 5 minutes | **Cooking** 0 minutes

1 tablespoon fresh ginger, grated or zested fine

½ cup Miso Base

¾ cup peanut butter

Juice of 2 limes (about 3 tablespoons)

2 tablespoons rice vinegar

2 tablespoons coconut cream

TIP

For a coconut cream substitute, use the solids from a can of coconut milk.

We debated giving peanut sauce its own section in the cookbook because it's the sideline star of so many of our favourite recipes: Thai barbecue chicken, salad rolls, veggie bowls and stir-fries. The rich and nutty notes add a highlight to light and fresh foods. And it instantly transports us back to our younger selves backpacking around the chaotic humidity of Southeast Asia.

1. Add all the ingredients to a blender or food processor. Blend on high until smooth and creamy, about 1 minute.

SPINACH GOMAE
MISO

Serves 4 | **Prep** 10 minutes | **Cooking** 10 minutes

1 cup frozen spinach

¼ cup peanut sauce

¼ cup toasted sesame seeds

These days our favourite application of peanut sauce is on spinach gomae. It's Josie's go-to any time we have sushi. So while our other favourite peanut sauce recipes are on our website, we decided to include the instructions for a quick spinach gomae here.

1. A couple hours ahead of time, set spinach out to thaw. If pressed for time, add frozen spinach and a cup of water to a pot, heat until thawed and strain off the water.
2. Squeeze the spinach to remove all excess water. You can use your hand or a spatula.
3. Divide the spinach into four and roll each into a ball.
4. Top each ball with 1 tablespoon of peanut sauce and sprinkle with 1 tablespoon of sesame seeds.

MUSHROOM GRAVY
MISO

Serves 4 | **Prep** 10 minutes | **Cooking** 20 minutes

1 cup onions, chopped fine

3 tablespoon olive oil

2½ cups mushrooms, sliced into slabs

1 teaspoon dried rosemary or 2 tablespoons fresh rosemary

1 teaspoon poultry seasoning

¼ cup red wine or 2 tablespoons red wine vinegar

2 cups Miso Base

2 tablespoons agar agar powder or cornstarch

Salt and pepper to taste

Often making a favourite food a little healthier means sacrificing flavour. This is not one of those recipes. If anything, this vegan gravy is better than any meat-based one we've tried. The wine-soaked mushrooms explode with juiciness and the liquid combines the best of a rich ramen broth with the satisfying depth of homemade turkey gravy. Pour it over pasta and roast chicken, dip bread in it and, of course, drown potatoes.

1. Warm a frying pan over medium heat. Add olive oil and onions and cook, stirring regularly, until they start to turn translucent. Add the rosemary and poultry seasoning and stir well. Add the mushrooms and stir some more.

2. Once the mushrooms get soft and wet looking, pour in the wine and Miso Base, then the agar agar. Keep stirring regularly.

3. Once the gravy is boiling, add salt and pepper to taste and serve immediately.

CAESAR
DRESSING

BASE
CAESAR DRESSING

Makes 1½ cups | **Prep** 10 minutes | **Cooking** 0 minutes

⅓ cup Parmesan cheese

2 eggs

⅓ cup olive oil

3 tablespoons fresh lemon juice (about one lemon)

1 tablespoon Worcestershire sauce

1 large garlic clove

1 teaspoon Dijon mustard

⅛ teaspoon anchovy paste

½ teaspoon salt

1 teaspoon peppercorns

SUBSTITUTION

For a vegan Caesar, ditch the Worcestershire and anchovy paste and add 1 tablespoon of miso paste.

TIP

If you need it to be celiac-friendly and can't find a gluten-free Worcestershire, omit it and add a sprinkle more anchovy paste.

Caesar is the most popular dressing at our house. We use it on salad, obviously, but also on Brussels sprouts, asparagus and sandwiches. Something about its creamy, tangy goodness is hard to beat. But, as we've found in a lot of sauces and dressings, hidden inside most store-bought and restaurant-made versions are a lot of dairy, low-quality oils, sugar and, most surprisingly, wheat. Worcestershire sauce, often known by the original brand name Lea & Perrins, is a key ingredient that adds rich umami flavour to most Caesar dressings. However, most Worcestershire, including Lea & Perrins, contains malt vinegar, which has enough wheat to bother celiacs. (FYI, it also contains fish sauce, so even if you ditch the traditional anchovy paste, Caesar is not usually vegetarian.)

Rather than give up on Caesar, we developed our own, celiac-friendly and healthy version. Emulsifying eggs and oil, plus adding generous quantities of Parmesan, creates enough creaminess to ditch milk ingredients. We eliminated sugars and fillers by using quality ingredients: mustard, oil and fresh lemon juice. A replacement for Lea & Perrins proved tougher, but we eventually found Wizard's, a gluten-free Worcestershire sauce that does the trick. This recipe is super-creamy and rich, with a nice bite that's perfect with salad and veggies.

1. Break Parmesan into half-inch cubes to help with blending.
2. Add all the ingredients into a blender container. Blend on high until the dressing becomes creamy, smooth and chunk-free.
3. Refrigerate. Keeps up to five days.

DECONSTRUCTED SALAD
CAESAR DRESSING

Serves 4 meal-sized salads | **Prep** 15 minutes | **Cooking** 0 minutes

1 big head romaine lettuce
or 3 romaine hearts

4 strips cooked bacon
or prosciutto ham

¼ cup giant capers

¼ cup Parmesan
cheese, grated thick

½ cup Caesar Dressing Base

pepper to taste

We like a good tossed salad, but when company is over and we're serving leafy greens as a main, we like to get fancy. Rather than dress it up, though, we take it apart. Full-sized romaine leaves, decorated with bacon, capers and shavings of Parmesan, look beautiful and change the whole experience of eating salad. Instead of shovelling it in, we're using a knife and fork to savour each oversized element. Instead of a universal serving, it's customizable for picky eaters. Instead of another side salad, it's something special and unique.

1. Disassemble the lettuce head, keeping the leaves intact. Wash and dry, then choose the 20 nicest leaves and arrange five per plate.
2. Chop bacon or prosciutto into bite-sized pieces.
3. Divide capers, cheese and bacon into four equal portions and arrange on the lettuce leaves.
4. Drizzle the deconstructed salad with a generous amount of Caesar Dressing Base. Grind fresh pepper over top.
5. Serve to critical acclaim.

DIP
CAESAR DRESSING

Serves 4 | **Prep** 10 minutes | **Cooking** 0 minutes

¼ cup Caesar Dressing Base

¼ cup plain 2% yogurt
(non-dairy works, too)

1 teaspoon lemon zest

3 cups mixed raw vegetables
(try carrots, cucumbers, celery,
red and orange peppers)

There is something very satisfying about eating with your hands. It probably tickles some ancient memory from our pre-fork and -spoon days. It's also great for lessening cleanup, which is probably the reason why veggies and dip make a popular party snack. So you won't surprise them with the veggies, but you can surprise them with the dip choice. Instead of the tried-and-stale ranch, dill or houmous, Caesar brings a surprising hit of sophistication and tangy zip to your guests' hands and mouths.

1. Combine Caesar Dressing Base and yogurt in a bowl. Stir well to combine.
2. Sprinkle lemon zest on top.
3. Cut an assortment of vegetables into hand-held chunks.
4. Dip and enjoy.

BRUSSELS SPROUTS
CAESAR DRESSING

Serves 4 | **Prep** 10 minutes | **Cooking** 35 minutes

1 pound Brussels sprouts, cut in half

1 tablespoon avocado oil

1 tablespoon balsamic reduction

2 tablespoons Caesar Dressing Base

2 strips cooked bacon, cut into chunks (optional)

There are two types of people in the world: Those who love Brussels sprouts any way they come and those who hate them until they try them like this: roasted and coated in Caesar dressing. The light char from a hot oven brings out a popcorn-like nuttiness that's far superior to boiled cabbage. The Caesar dressing adds a rich creaminess. It's a combo that has flipped more than one hater. You may want to double the recipe.

1.   Preheat the oven to 400°F. Line a baking sheet with parchment paper.

2.   Toss cleaned and cut Brussels sprouts in a big bowl with oil and vinegar. Transfer to the baking sheet, spreading sprouts into one layer.

3.   Bake in the oven for 20 minutes. (Air fry is even better.) Flip the Brussels sprouts and return to the oven for 15 minutes more, or until their outer leaves just start to char and turn brown.

4.   Return the sprouts to the big bowl. Pour on the Caesar Dressing Base and, if using, add the cooked bacon bits. Toss it all together and serve.

LEMON
PRESERVE

BASE
LEMON PRESERVE

Makes 1 cup | **Prep** 5 minutes | **Cooking** 15 minutes

2 large organic lemons

¼ cup lemon juice (from the fruit or store-bought juice)

¼ cup white wine (any variety will do, but we like Sauvignon Blanc)

3 teaspoons salt

TIP

We use Lemon Preserve Base just about everywhere we use lemon juice to add a more interesting and complex flavour. Just do us a favour and splurge on organic lemons. Non-organic ones often have a wax on the peel that will ruin the flavour.

NOTE

The recipe produces chunks of rind and creamy liquid. Some recipes call for the combination, while others are more specific.

Lemon Preserve Base is like an X-ACTO knife: you can live without it, but when you have it handy you will use it all the time. The wine and salt in this recipe add a complexity that takes the already versatile and cheerful yellow fruit to another level.

Add a little sparkling water to create a zesty mocktail. Mix it with chicken stock to make a lemony sauce. Or add it to salad dressings for a puckering kick. The preserve is quick and easy to make, and once it's in the fridge it keeps for about two weeks, so there's plenty of time to discover many other uses for it.

There is science behind the lemon's lovability. The acid in its juice makes fat and oils feel lighter and more digestible. Lemons are rich in antioxidants and Vitamin C. And we think they taste like a bite of sunshine.

1. Wash the lemons and slice them into thin rounds. Cut the rounds in half.

2. Add lemon slices to a Dutch oven or heavy pan with all the other ingredients. Stir to combine.

3. On high heat, bring the mixture to a boil. Cover with a tight-fitting lid and turn heat down to low.

4. Simmer for 12 minutes or until the liquid has reduced by half.

5. Use it right away or store in the refrigerator for two weeks.

ROASTED VEGGIE AND PECAN SALAD
LEMON PRESERVE

Serves 4 as a main | **Prep** 15 minutes | **Cooking** 25 minutes

DRESSING

¼ cup yogurt

¼ cup tahini

¼ cup water

1 tablespoon Lemon Preserve Base (rind and cream)

1 tablespoon honey

SALAD

2 cups butternut squash

2 sweet potatoes

3 carrots

2 potatoes

1 onion

2 pears

2 tablespoons avocado oil

1 teaspoon salt

1 tablespoon sriracha powder or sauce

1 orange, zested and juiced

2 tablespoons balsamic reduction

¼ cup roasted pecans

Fresh parsley or basil as garnish

This salad has a lot going for it. The mix of ingredients makes it naturally colourful and varied in flavour. Since just about any veggie will work, it's a great way to clean out your crisper. The ingredients are generally budget friendly. And it's satisfying. With the sweetness of the pears and umami from the tahini in the dressing, that's all five tastes: sweet, sour, bitter, salty and umami. A complete dinner, like this, feels more filling and reduces cravings for "a little something" later on.

1. Peel the squash and cut all the veggies and fruit. To ensure even cooking, cut the hard ingredients (squash, potatoes, carrots) into smaller pieces and the softer ones (onion, pears) into bigger chunks.

2. In a big bowl mix oil, salt, sriracha, orange juice and zest, and balsamic vinegar. Add the cut vegetables and mix well. Marinate for 10 to 15 minutes.

3. Preheat the oven to 400°F. Line a baking pan with parchment paper.

4. While the veggies marinate, make the dressing. Add all the dressing ingredients to a blender. Pulse on high until smooth and then set aside.

5. Spread marinated vegetables on the baking sheet. Place in the oven and roast for about 25 minutes.

6. Veggies are done when golden brown and everything is soft enough to poke with a fork. Remove from the oven and toss in a salad bowl with the pecans. Pour dressing over top and toss.

TEQUILA SOUR
LEMON PRESERVE

Serves 1 | **Prep** 5 minutes | **Cooking** 0 minutes

1 egg white, about ¾ ounce

1 ounce tequila

¾ ounce orange juice or lemon juice (fresh is best)

1 teaspoon Lemon Preserve Base (rind and cream)

If you love sour cocktails or classic margaritas, you will love this drink. If you like them both, this deliciously refreshing and super-smooth mix might become your new favourite. But first you need to overcome any reluctance to raw egg whites. We understand the concern, but there's nothing eggy about this recipe and, as long as you don't leave this drink sitting around - which you won't - it's food safe.

The key to this easy sipper is a double shake: first with no ice to work the egg whites into a thick froth, and then with ice to cool it down. The creamy egg whites contrast with the salty tang of the Lemon Preserve Base and both complement the funk of tequila. It's a dream team for warm-weather sipping.

1. Pour all the ingredients into a martini shaker, but don't add any ice.
2. Shake vigorously for 30 seconds.
3. Now fill the shaker half full with ice. Shake for another 20 seconds or so.
4. Add ice to a cocktail glass. Strain the lemon-tequila sour mix into the glass.
5. Garnish with a lemon or orange twist. Enjoy immediately.

POTATOES
LEMON PRESERVE

Serves 4 as a side | **Prep** 15 minutes | **Cooking** 50 minutes

10 Yukon Gold potatoes, peeled and cut into wedges

1 cup water

⅓ cup olive oil

1 tablespoon Lemon Preserve Base (rind and cream)

1 tablespoon Dijon mustard

1 teaspoon oregano

¼ teaspoon salt

½ teaspoon pepper

There are some things best left to the pros, like major electrical jobs, moving pianos and Pad Thai. Greek lemon potatoes used to be another one. We could never make them taste anywhere near as good as they taste in a restaurant – until we discovered the secret cooking technique and added our Lemon Preserve Base. The result was an instant classic. Crispy, buttery soft and lemony all in the same bite: it is now our favourite way to eat potatoes.

Be warned: this recipe will make a mess of whatever pan you use for roasting, but also know it cleans up more easily than expected. Just add hot water and leave it to soak for 30 minutes. In our opinion, a little scrubbing is totally worth it.

1. Preheat the oven to 375°F.
2. Place the potato wedges in a single layer in a high-sided baking pan or casserole dish.
3. In a bowl or measuring cup, combine all the other ingredients.
4. Pour the liquid over the potato wedges. The liquid should almost cover the potatoes.
5. Put the pan in the oven and bake for 30 minutes.
6. Flip potatoes and return them to the oven for another 15 to 20 minutes.
7. They are done when most of the liquid has boiled off and the potatoes are golden and crispy on the outside and you can easily spike them with a fork.

HALIBUT
LEMON PRESERVE

Serves 4 | **Prep** 5 minutes | **Cooking** 12 minutes

700 to 900 grams (1.5 to 2 pounds) halibut fillet

2 tablespoons Lemon Preserve Base cream

2 tablespoons olive oil

Salt and pepper to taste

There's nothing delicate about a living and flopping halibut. Hauling one into a fishing boat is always an exciting experience. Halibut's delicate white meat is another story: it's easily overcooked, dried out and overpowered. That's one of the reasons we like this recipe. We find basting the fish in oil helps the meat stay moist, while the Lemon Preserve Base adds fresh and vibrant flavours that complement any seafood.

You can cook halibut in the oven, but we think the smokiness of the barbecue adds a *je ne sais quoi* that takes it to the next level. Serve with a green salad and maybe some fresh asparagus. Just writing this reminds us of warm summer nights.

1. Preheat a barbecue to 400°F. (If you don't have a thermometer, just shy of full throttle.)
2. Wash and dry the halibut fillets.
3. In a bowl, mix the Lemon Preserve Base and oil. Spread onto the flesh side of the halibut. Sprinkle with salt and pepper.
4. Place the fish on a piece of tinfoil and cook on the barbecue for 12 minutes. It's done when you poke the thinnest part of the meat with a fork and it just starts to flake.

GRILLED EGGPLANT
LEMON PRESERVE

Serves 4 | **Prep** 15 minutes + 30 minutes of salting | **Cooking** 10 minutes

1 eggplant (we like the Japanese variety)

1 teaspoon coarse salt

2 tablespoons olive oil

⅓ cup full-fat yogurt

1 tablespoon Lemon Preserve Base cream

1 tablespoon balsamic reduction

¼ cup roasted pistachios

1 teaspoon dried rose petals (optional decoration)

1 tablespoon dried strawberries or figs (optional decoration)

TIP
—

We recommend salting the raw eggplant to remove some of the water, which yields a crisper result, but if you're in a rush you can skip this step.

Josie stumbled on this recipe almost by accident. We've long grilled eggplant slabs to make "noodles" for an all-veggie lasagna. They come out all crispy and gooey, and we gobble up any leftovers. With an eggplant and the Lemon Preserve Base in the fridge (and both nearing expiration), Josie took a chance. She mixed the Lemon Preserve Base with yogurt, threw on some pistachios for crunch and added rose petals for an artistic splash of colour and dried strawberries for a hint of sweet. With the first bite we knew we had a classic. It's easy, complex and has an interesting mouth feel.

1. Slice the eggplant lengthwise into long, thin strips.

2. Remove some of the water from the eggplant by sprinkling salt onto both sides of the slabs and laying them on a plate covered in paper towel. Let them sit for 30 minutes, flipping halfway through.

3. In a small bowl, mix the Lemon Preserve Base cream and yogurt.

4. Heat a grill on the stovetop or the barbecue to 400°F. (We prefer the open flame of a barbecue.) Oil it lightly with avocado oil.

5. Pat dry the eggplant slabs and coat them in olive oil.

6. Grill the eggplant for five minutes per side. They're done when the outside is tanned and getting crispy and the inside is soft and creamy. Remove them from heat and arrange on a serving plate.

7. Pour the yogurt-lemon dressing across the eggplant, drizzle balsamic vinegar over top and toss on the pistachios. If you want, decorate with rose petals and dried fruit.

8. Serve as a side. It's great with barbecued chicken and a Caesar salad.

CHICKEN
LEMON PRESERVE

Serves 4 | **Prep** 10 minutes | **Cooking** 35 minutes

4 boneless, skinless
chicken breasts

1 tablespoon avocado oil

2 cups chicken broth

3 tablespoons Lemon
Preserve Base cream

1 tablespoon agar agar
powder or cornstarch

1 tablespoon Miso Base

1 teaspoon dry mustard

Salt and pepper to taste

SUBSTITUTION

To cook a whole lemon chicken,
coat in Lemon Preserve Base,
put a whole lemon in the cavity
and roast in a 400°F oven until
a meat thermometer shows
the meat is cooked.

It's all about the sauce. Combining our Miso Base with our Lemon Preserve Base creates a rich, tangy and satisfying flavour that's enhanced with the chicken juices. Think gravy, but lighter and more complex. It's so good we literally drink it off our plate and clean the pot with our spoons.

With the two bases already prepped this is an easy recipe to make, leaving extra time to throw together a couple sides. Roast veggies are a good option. But definitely serve it with rice – mostly because it's another opportunity to soak up the sauce.

1. Heat a Dutch oven or heavy pot on the stovetop on medium-high. Test the heat by adding a droplet of water. You're ready to start when it sizzles.

2. Wash and dry the chicken breasts. Add the oil to the pot and swirl it around. Place the chicken breasts in the pot.

3. Brown chicken for 2 minutes. Flip and brown on the other side for another 2 minutes.

4. Turn the heat down to low and cover with a tight-fitting lid. Leave it to cook for 10 minutes.

5. Meanwhile, in a bowl combine chicken broth, Lemon Preserve Base, Miso Base, agar agar, mustard and salt and pepper. Whisk together until there are no lumps.

6. When the chicken has cooked for 10 minutes use a meat thermometer to check doneness. It may need to cook a little longer. When the meat hits 165°F, pour the sauce over the chicken. Stir and heat the sauce until it boils and thickens to your desired consistency.

7. Serve with rice and fresh lemon slices.

CASHEW
CREAM

Base **107**

Shrimp Salad **108**

Creamy Pasta Sauce **111**

Chipotle Sauce **112**

Raw Lemon "Cheesecake" with Raspberry Coulis **115**

Chocolate Truffle Cake **119**

BASE
CASHEW CREAM

Makes 2 cups | **Prep** 10 minutes + 30 minutes soaking time | **Cooking** 0 minutes

2 cups raw cashew pieces

¾ cup cold water

¼ teaspoon salt

TIP
—

Whole cashews work for this recipe, but the pieces absorb water faster, blend more easily and are less expensive.

If you're making one of our desserts and want more for another recipe, you should double this recipe.

Cashew cream is an amazing building block, especially if you're trying to cut dairy from your diet. It stands in brilliantly for whipped cream, yogurt, cream cheese, sour cream and more.

It's often a healthier alternative. Cashews are a good source of fibre, which slows the absorption of sugar. That makes them especially good in sweet desserts, where they'll reduce sugar spikes. They're full of magnesium, a key component of muscle function and relaxation. And they contain nearly the same amount of protein as cooked meats. With plentiful good fats, they are filling without lots of calories.

However you use our Cashew Cream Base, few will suspect the gourmet result is vegan and healthy. Our advice: don't burst their bubble.

1. Put the cashew pieces in a measuring cup and add the water. The water should just cover the cashews. If it doesn't, add a little more. Leave the cashews to soak for at least 30 minutes, until they grow large and soft.

2. Pour the cashews and leftover water into a blender and add salt. Blend on high power. You will need to mash the mixture and probably scrape the sides at least once. You're aiming for a smooth and creamy texture that just barely pours. If it's too thick, add extra water, one teaspoon at a time.

3. Use it right away or refrigerate for up to a week.

SHRIMP SALAD
CASHEW CREAM

Serves 4 | **Prep** 10 minutes | **Cooking** 0 minutes

SALAD

100 grams small
cooked shrimp

½ teaspoon lemon juice

1 pink grapefruit,
skinned and sliced

½ an avocado

DRESSING

2 tablespoons Cashew
Cream Base

2 tablespoons cream from
Lemon Preserve Base (or 3
tablespoons lemon juice
and ½ teaspoon salt)

Salads are like art. Combine the textures, shapes, colours and sizes just right and they're beautiful to look at – and eat. To us, this salad is a masterpiece. The shrimp, grapefruit and avocado complement each other in texture, shape, colour and size. The creamy, tart dressing brings the flavours together.

It's highly adaptable, too. In the summer, we like to eat it on lettuce. As a side salad, it's refreshing and light. In the winter, we prefer it on top of rice. As a meal, it's warm and substantial. Either way, it's fast and easy to whip up, but looks far more involved.

1. In a small bowl, mix shrimp and lemon juice and set aside.
2. In another bowl, combine the Cashew Cream Base and Lemon Preserve Base and mix well.
3. Peel the grapefruit. Slice into slabs and cut into quarters.
4. Peel the skin off the half avocado and slice the fruit into strips.
5. Get artsy and moody with how you serve it.
6. Drizzle with lemon-cashew dressing.
7. Devour.

CREAMY PASTA SAUCE
CASHEW CREAM

Serves 4 | **Prep** 5 minutes | **Cooking** 20 minutes

1 onion, chopped into small pieces

1 tablespoon olive oil

½ cup white wine

1 cup Cashew Cream Base (page 107)

½ cup Miso Base (page 65)

3 tablespoons lemon juice (about 1 lemon)

½ cup nutritional yeast

1 teaspoon garlic salt

½ teaspoon pepper

¼ teaspoon salt

300 grams of chicken, cooked and cut into bite-sized pieces (optional)

SUBSTITUTION

Along with Cashew Cream Base, we use our Miso Base in this recipe. It whips together quickly, but you can use an equivalent amount of veggie or chicken broth.

Think of this velvety sauce as a vegan love child of mac and cheese and Alfredo. It emerged when our daughter developed a dairy intolerance, but still craved creamy pasta. Nutritional yeast and Cashew Cream Base combine to deliver a near-dairy creaminess, a cheese-like flavour and comfort-food richness. The wine and miso add a nuanced complexity that teases more sophisticated palates. With chicken and a salad, it's a great multi-generational meal.

1. Heat a frying pan over medium heat. Add the olive oil and onion and stir well. Fry the onion, stirring often, until it turns translucent. (This is a good time to start boiling the water for the pasta.)

2. Once the onion is cooked, turn the heat to low. Add the white wine and Cashew Cream Base and stir to combine. Add the Miso Base and stir until the sauce has a uniform consistency.

3. Continue adding the other ingredients, one by one, whisking and stirring until well mixed.

4. Aim for a thick but still runny consistency. If it's too thick, add more wine, one tablespoon at a time.

5. Once all the ingredients are whisked in, add the meat (optional) and turn the heat up to medium. Cook, stirring often, until the sauce bubbles.

6. Either mix in your favourite cooked pasta, stirring and tossing to coat each noodle, or plate the pasta and add the sauce on top.

CHIPOTLE SAUCE
CASHEW CREAM

Makes a lot | **Prep** 5 minutes | **Cooking** 0 minutes

½ cup Cashew Cream Base

2 tablespoons chipotles, peppers and sauce

2 tablespoons orange juice

½ teaspoon salt

TIP

These ratios produce a medium heat. Adjust the amount of chipotle to your desired spiciness.

I (Ryan) am a sucker for any Mexican-influenced food, but especially anything containing chipotle. The smokey heat hits all the right taste buds. The key is chipotle peppers: they come in a can fully spiced and pickled. Here, we've combined them with our Cashew Cream Base and tart lemon juice to create a fiery sauce that goes well with a startling variety of foods. You can slather it on steamed corn or roasted vegetables. And it's perfect on top of all kinds of tacos and burritos. This recipe makes a lot, but we know you'll find a use for it.

1. Place all the ingredients in a blender and blend until smooth and consistent in colour.
2. Serve liberally and regularly.

RAW LEMON "CHEESECAKE" WITH RASPBERRY COULIS
CASHEW CREAM

Serves 8 | **Prep** 30 minutes | **Cooking** 0 but 1 hour of chilling time

CRUST

2 cups almond meal

1 teaspoon cinnamon

⅛ teaspoon salt

3 tablespoons coconut oil

2 tablespoons cold water

1 tablespoon maple syrup

FILLING

4 lemon slices from
Lemon Preserve

1 teaspoon guar gum

¼ cup white chocolate chips

2 cups Cashew Cream Base

¼ cup and 1 tablespoon
xylitol or sugar

1 teaspoon vanilla

pinch of salt

Does it count as dessert if it is good for you? Don't waste too much time pondering this philosophical question and just savour this incredibly tasty and healthy play on a vegan cheesecake. That's right, no dairy *and* low carb and little sugar. It's even raw. Yet it's still rich, indulgent and a little intense - just like any good cheesecake should be.

The biggest difference between an authentic cheesecake and this raw version is the time required. Real cheesecake takes hours. This one comes together much faster, though it still requires some planning. You need to make the Cashew Cream Base and Lemon Preserve Base and, after assembly, the cake needs to chill for an hour to firm up. But the hands-on part takes less than 20 minutes, including making the raspberry coulis topping. That's time well spent for this delectable investment.

1. Start with the crust. Combine all the dry crust ingredients in a big bowl and mix. Add the water and oil. Mix with your hands until you can make the dough into a big ball. If it is too dry, add more water, a half teaspoon at a time.

2. In a 7-inch-diameter cheesecake pan, or similar-sized cake pan, add the crust mixture and smooth it flat with your hands until it covers the bottom of the pan.

3. Place white chocolate chips in a microwave-safe dish. Microwave for 30 seconds; stir and add 15 more seconds until it turns to liquid.

recipe continues

recipe continued from previous page

RASPBERRY COULIS

2 cups frozen
raspberries, thawed

¼ cup maple syrup

1 teaspoon vanilla extract

3 tablespoons lemon juice
(about one lemon)

2 teaspoons guar gum

SUBSTITUTION

If you don't have Lemon
Preserve Base or just want an
alternative flavour, sub in ½
cup of juice and 2 tablespoons
of zest from any citrus fruit.
Our second favourite is lime.

1. To a food processor or blender, add the Lemon Preserve Base, melted white chocolate chips, Cashew Cream Base, sugar, vanilla and salt. Blend until creamy.

2. Pour the lemon cashew filling into the crust. Use a spatula to smooth it out.

3. Place the "cheesecake" in the freezer for an hour to allow it to set.

4. Start the coulis. After cleaning the blender, add all the raspberry coulis ingredients. Blend on high until smooth.

5. Refrigerate the coulis.

6. Ten minutes before serving, remove the "cheesecake" from the freezer and the coulis from the fridge to let them warm and soften.

7. Use the coulis like an icing and smother over the whole "cheesecake" or just pour over individual pieces.

CHOCOLATE TRUFFLE CAKE
CASHEW CREAM

Serves 10 | **Prep** 40 minutes | **Cooking** 0 but 1 hour in freezer

1 cup dark chocolate chips or chunks

2 cups Cashew Cream Base

½ cup + 1 tablespoon xylitol or sugar

⅓ cup cocoa powder

2 teaspoon vanilla

2 shots decaf espresso

1 teaspoon guar gum

TOPPING (OPTIONAL)

1 tablespoon dark cocoa powder

1 teaspoon flaked salt

pinch of chili powder

¼ cup chocolate-covered espresso beans

TIP

The key to a velvety texture is using a high quality, powerful blender.

This is a great party cake. It looks beautiful, tastes rich and creamy and everyone loves chocolate. Plus, because it's so decadent, a small piece will satisfy most eaters, so you can get away with an eight inch cake for a big crowd. Decorating the top elevates it further. We offer a suggestion, but a few berries and some candles will do the job nicely, too. Make it your own.

For the chocolate, use your favourite variety and/or whatever you have on hand: chips, chunks or a bar. We like dark and know that the better the quality, the better the result.

1. Melt the chocolate by adding it to a microwave-safe dish and heating it in a microwave in 15 second increments until it is all liquid. Add it to a blender.

2. To the blender add Cashew Cream Base, vanilla, cocoa powder, chili powder and xylitol.

3. Brew two shots of espresso. In a mug or bowl mix the coffee and guar gum. Add to the blender.

4. Blend everything until creamy and smooth. This can take a few goes, stirring and scraping the sides of the blender between pulses. Aim for a consistency that's thick, but still pourable. If it's too thick, add a little water.

5. Line an 7-inch cheesecake pan with parchment paper. Pour the batter mixture into the pan. Flatten the top with a spatula. Spinning the pan can help create a flat top.

6. Decorate liberally. We like fresh or frozen fruit, salt and chili powder, even chocolate covered espresso beans.

7. Place in the freezer for an hour or longer to firm up. Ten minutes before serving, remove from the freezer to soften.

ACKNOWLEDGEMENTS

Creating this cookbook reminds us of the process of making gluten-free sourdough bread. We found a recipe, mixed up the ingredients, let it rise and then rest and finally we baked it. The result was good, but we knew we could do better. We tweaked the ingredients and the directions and tried again. And again. Many iterations and several months later, we were finally happy with the bread we pulled out of the oven.

This cookbook involved a similar process of evolution and refinement. It just took a lot longer and was far more work. Where sourdough and this book diverged was in the support we received. We were mostly alone figuring out gluten-free sourdough – some even said it wasn't possible. But when it came to writing a cookbook we only received encouragement. Without that support there would be no *Habit*.

We have a lot of people to thank. Starting with our mothers, Myrna and Broda, for instilling a love of cooking and healthy eating. Michael has always been a quiet source of confidence and support. Our daughter Paige is our inspiration and always pushed us to get it done. There are all the other family and friends who tasted our recipes, cheered our progress and offered encouraging words, often when we needed it most.

Then there are the @restlessjosie followers on Instagram who gave us the courage to start and the energy to finish. There's a lot of talk about the ills of social media, but it is in supportive, loving communities like this that these platforms fulfill their promise.

We want to thank Jen Groundwater for her attention to detail throughout the editing and proofing process. She made the writing better in every way. Finally, this book would be a shadow of its potential if it wasn't for Lou Dahl. She's an amazing sister in-law, an incredible photographer and beautiful designer. She pushed us to do better and her touch helped us create something we're really proud of.

INDEX

Find this Pear and Gorgonzola Pizza on our website.
It uses our Salsa Verde Base (page 33 of this book).

Restless Josie

—— COOKS ——

www.restlessjosiecooks.com

Made in United States
Troutdale, OR
08/19/2024

22128412R00076